ding 0118 9015950
le 0118 9015100
ersham
KT-418-961
3412600061 9869

Warning!

Before you read this book you should know that biking *can* be dangerous. If you are not careful, and even sometimes if you are, you can break bones, including that hard skull that wraps up your brain. This book explains extreme biking, but is not intended to be used as a training manual. If you plan to try extreme biking protect yourself by using the right equipment and choosing trails, doing tricks, etc. that you're ready for.

A WORD ABOUT HELMETS: Some of the cyclists pictured in this book are not wearing helmets. We do not recommend this. We suggest that you wear a helmet whenever you get on a bike. But it's not just us—the laws of 17 states and over 70 localities **require** you to wear a helmet. It's your brain—take care of it.

If you do go out and break your head, or any other part of your body or anyone else's body, don't blame National Geographic. We told you to be careful!

(Translation into legalese: Neither the publisher nor the author shall be liable for any bodily harm that may be caused or sustained as a result of conducting any of the activities described in this book.)

One of the world's largest nonprofit scientific and educational organizations, the NATIONAL GEOGRAPHIC SOCIETY was founded in 1888 "for the increase and diffusion of geographic knowledge." Fulfilling this mission, the Society educates and inspires millions every day through its magazine, books, television programs, videos, maps and atlases, research grants, the National Geographic Bee, teacher workshops, and innovative classroom materials. The Society is supported through membership dues, charitable gifts, and income from the sale of its educational products. This support is vital to National Geographic's mission to increase global understanding and promote conservation of our planet through exploration, research, and education.

For more information, please call 1-800-NGS LINE (647-5463) or write to the following address:
National Geographic Society
1145 17th Street N.W.
Washington, D.C. 20036-4688 U.S.A.
Visit the Society's Web site at www

Reading Borough Council
3412600061 9869

NATIONAL GEOGRAPHIC

EXTREME Sports

BIKE!

Your Guide to Mountain Biking, BMX, Road and Fast-Track Racing, C-X Racing and more.

BY MONIQUE PETERSON
ZACHARY ZIMMERMAN

Illustrations Jack Dickason

NATIONAL GEOGRAPHIC
WASHINGTON, D.C.

What's Inside

Reinventing the Wheel

A mix of tradition and technology, the bicycle continues to spin in extreme directions. Which way do you wanna ride?

A bicycle stunt rider hangs in midair for a dirt-jumping exhibition at the X Games in San Francisco.

Here's a peek into some of the most intense experiences on two wheels.

Find out what it takes for cyclo-crossers to power across a muddy field or for mountain bikers to carve gnarly switchbacks. Get the skinny on how the pros go faster, climb higher, and claim the yellow jersey. Fly with the freestyle crowd as they renegotiate the laws of physics.

Whether you like the road, the track, the dirt, or the hills, this book is for you. It all starts with the love of the bike. From pro racers forging a new sport in the mud bogs of Belgium to suburban kids catching air like their favorite motorcycle heroes, they did more than just start new ways to ride—they added whole new sports to the bicycling pantheon.

From the Tour de France to the X Games, catch the spectacle that is modern biking.

Learn how they did it, what it takes to go to the limit—and change the rules for a new generation.

Extreme
Sports

Part One

Mountain Biking

the rivers, the big outdoors. Why not take your bike where it's never been before? Explore the world of mountain biking.

Ready to Roll

*Nothing compares to the adrenaline rush from ripping
down the road on your bike. Combine that with
a love of dirt, sky, and trees, and you're ready
for a ride that's pure adventure.*

Forget about traffic, stoplights,
and boring pavement. Say hello
to the big outdoors—once your
knobbies meet dirt, you're good to go.
Maybe this time you and your friends
will clear more hurdles, go faster,
and ride with more flair than ever
before. By now you're already hooked:
You live to ride, and ride to live.

HERE, THERE, ANYWHERE

You don't need a mountain in your backyard to go mountain biking. Mountain biking has come to mean virtually any off-road—and off-pavement—riding experience. You can be in North Carolina's Tsali wilderness, in a state park, or on a gravel fire road. Are you into extreme nature, like the slickrock trails of Moab, Utah? Maybe you prefer the thrill of a killer climb followed by extreme speed, or forging your own path in the backcountry, mastering roots, rocks, sand, and mud.

TAKE THE CHALLENGE

Depending on where—and when—you ride, the obstacles will be different. Your favorite trail in the woods can change dramatically each season. Fall leaves can cover rocks and roots. Mud can stay on the trail long after a rainfall and can really bog you down. Lush foliage that's present in the springtime may have died out by fall. Each time you ride, expect new challenges. And keep in mind that what's extreme for you may be a piece of cake for your best friend, and what's a cinch for you might be terrifying for the next person.

FREE YOUR MIND

The biggest challenge often has nothing to do with the trail and everything to do with how you approach the trail—your attitude. If you're not used to off-road riding, it may take a while to learn that your bike can and will go over obstacles without resulting in a flat tire or a face plant. But if you relax, enjoy the scenery, and maintain a positive outlook, before you know it, you'll be carving your way through the woods with a style all your own.

THE LINGO

SINGLE-TRACK: A narrow, one-way trail.

PORTAGE: To carry your bike through an unrideable section of the trail.

TECHNICAL: Terrain that requires a specific set of skills and techniques to navigate.

BUNNY HOP: To lift your wheels off the ground and clear obstacles while riding.

ENDO: To fly over the handlebars because you've flipped your bike end over end.

BONK: The sensation that happens when your body runs out of fuel. Warning: Can lead to endos and face plants.

FEATHER: To lightly squeeze and release the brake levers to control your speed.

WASHBOARD: A section of the trail with many ridges and ruts, usually caused by erosion.

FACE PLANT: Landing flat on your face.

BABY HEADS: Loose, skull-sized rocks on the trail.

KNOBBIES: Tires specially designed with patterned knobs to improve traction for off-road riding.

SNAKEBITE: A flat that occurs when the inner tube is pinched between an obstacle and the wheel rim, often due to an underinflated tire. So called because the parallel tears look like fang punctures.

Bring It On

Remember that first bike ride? You could travel farther and faster by yourself than ever before. Along with the thrill of accomplishment, you discovered a new kind of freedom.

So now you know how to ride a bike. You've always liked to go fast and see how far over you can lean in a turn, but there's something new. Now you like to ride over rocks or roots and in between trees, and you're not happy unless you're covered with dirt and have to scrape the bugs off your teeth. You've caught a fever, and it's called mountain biking.

DON'T LEAVE HOME WITHOUT 'EM

HELMET: Should fit snugly on your head.

GLOVES: For protection and comfort.

EYESHIELDS: Ever get a bug in your eye at 15 mph?

WATER BOTTLE(S): Avoid sunstroke! You can sweat a quart of water an hour during a challenging ride.

FIRST-AID KIT: Should contain sterile pads, surgical tape, antibiotic ointments, and an antiseptic cleanser.

TIRE PATCH KIT: So you don't have to walk home.

AIR PUMP: A patch kit is useless without one.

TOOL KIT: A good one should include a chain breaker, various wrenches, Allen keys, and a Phillips screwdriver.

GOTTA LOVE THE GEAR

Three styles of mountain bikes and biking have evolved.

CROSS COUNTRY: These light bikes are designed for longer rides, better climbs, and faster sprints. The most common design is the "hardtail" with a front fork and two to three inches of suspension.

FREERIDE: Generally heavier and with a stronger frame, freeride bikes can handle steeper, more treacherous descents at the cost of climbing ability. Five inches of rear suspension and four up front are normal, enabling the freerider to "bomb" obstacles and drop-offs while maintaining speed.

DOWNHILL: These heavy monster bikes have the most suspension front and rear, and are geared for high-speed descents. Special chain guards keep the chain from jumping off the front chainring and possibly causing an accident. Flat pedals let riders use their feet to "dab" the ground during a turn. Because of extra risks involved, downhillers wear more protective gear: full face helmets, abrasion-resistant clothes, plastic body armor, and shin guards.

PROPER RESPECT

The more attention you give your bike, the longer it will last and the better it'll ride. Periodically, clean and lubricate the chain and exposed cables, especially after a muddy ride, and clean out any gunk you find between the chainrings. Check for bent or broken spokes in the wheels. They can cause the wheel rim to go out of true and rub against the brake pad. If you crash during a ride, thoroughly check the bike before you ride it again. Make sure the tires haven't been punctured, the brakes are operating properly, gears shift smoothly, the handlebar is on tightly, and the frame is free of dents or cracks.

The aluminum frame of this full-suspension mountain bike is designed to add strength and cut down on weight.

Get in the Groove

Single-track unfolding beneath a canopy of trees, a hardpack fire road dropping into the river valley below, a twisting staircase of roots and rocks: They all lure you in with the promise of challenge and beauty.

Your style of riding can be heavily influenced by the landscape where you ride. The northeastern United States is known for its "technical" riding with its rocky soil, lush vegetation, and gnarled roots. Riding smoothly requires the ability to hop over logs and fallen branches as well as finesse your tires through fallen leaves and over slippery rocks. Drier climates, such as southern California and the western slope of Colorado, demand the ability to negotiate between hardpack and loose, granular soil.

RIDE LOOSE

All essential bike handling skills stem from the ability to shift your weight rapidly and smoothly. When you're climbing, spread your weight over the front wheel to keep it firmly on the ground. Try to pedal in smooth circles for sustained power. During a descent, you'll want to get off the saddle and move your weight back, sometimes to the point where your stomach is over the seat, and keep your arms slightly bent for shock absorption. To cut sharp turns, ride with your inside pedal high and move your weight onto the outside pedal. Learn how to loosen your mind as well as your body. Ride smoothly, instead of quickly, and you'll naturally gain speed.

MASTERING THE ESSENTIALS

THE BUNNY HOP *An invaluable tool when a root or rock is in your path and you'd much rather sail over it than stop and dismount. Practice with a soda can and work your way up to larger obstacles.*

STEP 1. Make sure you're riding with enough speed to carry your bike over the can. For maximum smoothness, stop pedaling when you're two bike lengths from the can.

STEP 2. Rise up out of the seat with your legs slightly bent at the knee and center your weight over the bike.

STEP 3. When you're one bike length from the can, compress your weight on the bike, pushing it into the ground. You should end the movement with arms and legs fully bent and your upper body close to the bike. Think of a cat ready to pounce.

STEP 4. Spring straight up using your legs without jerking your arms. Both tires should come off the ground at the same time. As soon as they do, pull your legs up (this is easier with toe clips or clipless pedals), allowing the bike to rise higher.

STEP 5. Keep your front wheel straight as you come in for a landing.

CLEARING AN OBSTACLE *Say there's a log in your way and it's too big to bunny hop. This move uses elements of the bunny hop but involves lifting the front and rear wheels separately.*

STEP 1. Assess your speed. You want to go slower than when you bunny hop but fast enough to keep your momentum.

STEP 2. When you're one wheel length away, move your weight forward and compress your weight, then pull up on the front wheel while you slide your weight back. Simultaneously, push down on your pedals to give you lift, then pause your pedaling.

STEP 3. When your front wheel goes over the log, throw the bike forward, extending your arms. You should be out of the seat when your rear wheel hits the log. Pedal to keep your momentum.

STEP 4. Keep the front wheel straight and your arms extended but slightly bent. When the front wheel hits the ground on the other side, your rear wheel should be on top of the log or dropping off the other side. Your weight is back, and you're looking good.

Extreme Conditions

Who says mountain biking is a fair-weather sport? Die-hards don't stop with a little rain, snow, mud, or sleet. They don't even need daylight. With the right gear and some technical know-how, you can make mountain biking a year-round, round-the-clock sport.

Sure, there's nothing like a sunny summer day bunny hopping over creeks and logs, grinding in your granny gear up Impossible Hill, and finally collapsing at the top, legs like rubber, with a silly grin from ear to ear. But are you ready to take it to a new level? Riding in the snow, at night, or in inclement conditions can turn an extreme trail into the wildest ride of your life.

ICE IS NICE

You don't have to be a Winter X Games biker to rip down slalom runs, carve S's in the snow, and feel the crunch of ice under your tires—but it wouldn't hurt. Snow riding makes biking feel like an entirely different sport. It's easier to take risks in the snow because you know you'll have a soft landing if you fall. If the snow is very loose or powdery you may sink too deep to ride, but if it's hard-packed, granular, or icy, get ready for some of the most challenging and fun rides ever. To maximize traction, snow riders insert screws in their tires or use specially studded snow tires. And winter riding can make you a champion, come springtime. Not only will you get a surge in confidence, but you'll be a better and fitter rider.

Take a tip from those in the know: Momentum is your friend. If you can keep your back wheel turning and maintain traction, you'll have a much easier time forging your path.

LUNACY

Can't get enough of your favorite trail? Do it in the dark. A trail you thought you knew like the back of your hand can look and feel totally different at night. Even with a full moon, super-charged headlamps, and handlebar lights, the trail will look different from what you might expect. Shadows can be misleading, and distance can be hard to judge. Washboards and depressions in the road can come up unexpectedly, bringing you ever closer to something that really does go bump in the night.

MUD, SLUDGE, AND GRUNGE

Some areas, like Vermont, have a mud season after the winter snowmelt. Getting out on the trail means getting into guck and goo—and lots of it. Fine layers of silt can cover up rocks, making the terrain slick and easy to spin out on. Mud on a trail can be deeper than it looks. What seems easy to ride through can suck your tires—and your energy—right into the thick of it. Tire choice can be especially important in these conditions. If you know you'll be riding in the mud, use a slightly narrower tire, like a CX tire (see p. 53), with widely spaced knobs to allow the wet stuff to flow through.

RULES FOR THE RUGGED

1. RIDE WITH YOUR POSSE. Always plan to take on the rough stuff with experienced friends. You'll share a ride, as well as equipment, food, and support.

2. PREPARE TO STOP. If your rims get wet or frozen, you can pretty much forget about using your brakes. Clean your rims to keep a good braking surface. Learn how to shift gears to slow down, use a foot to brake, and dismount while your bike is rolling.

3. LAYER IT. In the wet, cold, or both, dress in layers for greatest comfort. Make sure your outer layer is a waterproof, breathable shell.

Kick It into Gear

You're chasing the tire in front of you, dirt kicking up into your face. Your legs feel like lead, yet you keep them spinning. You drop off a small ledge and shift gears to attack the hill. You're smiling because you love to race.

Not long after the first mountain bike races down the Repack Trail in Marin County, California, in the mid-1970s, other organized races and non-competitive events began to emerge to test the limits of those early enthusiasts. They included courses like the Road Apple Rally in New Mexico and the Pearl Pass Tour from Crested Butte to Aspen, Colorado, and finally the first mountain bike world championship held in Durango, Colorado, in 1990. Now mountain bike races push the envelope with long- and short-course, cross-country events, blistering downhill and dual slalom courses, and twenty-four-hour team relay events such as the famous Twenty-Four Hours of Moab.

THE RACING FOLKS

The National Off-Road Bicycle Association (NORBA) is the premier mountain bike racing organization in the United States. Pro and amateur riders participate in more than a thousand NORBA events per year, including the American Mountain Bike Challenge and the Junior Olympic Mountain Bike Series for younger riders.

PLANET X

In 1995, more than 350 of the world's most extreme athletes gathered in Rhode Island for the first ever Extreme Games, now known as the X Games. In these annual competitions, mountain bikers join the ranks of skiboarders, ice climbers, and snowboarders in a competition for the title of Most Extreme Athlete on the Planet. At the Winter X Games, the most extreme downhill event goes to the snow mountain bikers, geared up in aerodynamic body suits, who race down slalom courses at speeds up to 70 miles per hour!

CRÈME DE LA CRÈME

The world's best mountain bikers know the events not to miss are the World Championships, the Olympics, and the World Cup. The one-day World Championship race pits riders from around the globe against each other in super intense downhill speedfests as well as through cross-country courses built by some of the world's most extreme mountain bikers. Mountain biking became an official Olympic sport in 1996, making it possible for the first time to go for the gold. Even more grueling than the Olympics is the World Cup, a series of eight races held in some of the most amazing mountain biking meccas around the world.

DEADLY NEDLY

After more than 20 years in competition, mountain bike legend Ned Overend is admired both as a great champion of the sport (his prizes include several World Cup wins and six national titles) and for his spirit as he continues to win races despite "retiring" in 1996 at age 41. He continues to compete because of his love of the sport and his ability to mix fun with the hard efforts of racing.

RUTHIE MATTHES

Former World Champion, member of the 2000 U.S. Olympic team, 1992 World Cup champion, and national cross-country champion from 1996 to 1998, Ruthie Matthes is truly a world-class athlete. Matthes started racing road bikes in her home state of Idaho at age 17, but she didn't really start mountain biking until nearly ten years later. Since then, this biker chick with the unforgettable smile has been in just about every major mountain biking competition the sport has to offer. Her words to the wise: Be a team player! Support local bike organizations and pitch in to maintain trails and keep them debris-free.

BMX Biking

Who says you can't teach an old dog new tricks? Bikes called 20-inchers introduce something new to a sport that's been around the track. Go vertical, work the dirt circuit. Welcome to BMX.

The 20-Inch Revolution

Think of flying off ramps, hairpin curves, double and triple jumps, mud holes, wheelies, and edging out riders in a mad dash to the finish line. Think of doing it all with small wheels and a single gear, and you're thinking BMX.

BMX, or bicycle motocross, owes its origins to dirt motorcycle racing enthusiasts. Kids got pumped up to ride their bicycles on courses that let them imitate their favorite motorcycle heroes. In 1970, 13-year-old Scot Breithaupt organized the first neighborhood BMX races in Long Beach, California. Thirty-five riders came for the first race and paid a quarter to enter. The next weekend, 150 kids showed up. Within a few years, BMX racing had become a nationally sanctioned sport.

MOTO MOJO

It all starts on the dirt track. A pack of riders line up behind the starting gate, wait for the signal, and then tear through a winding course filled with jumps, dips, berms, and turns. The first racer to cross the finish line wins the heat, or moto. Riders compete in three motos; the rider with best two out of three is the winner. Racers generally compete against other riders in the same skill category (beginner, novice, expert) and age group (5–19, 19-and-up). Once riders win eight races within a calendar year, they can advance to the next skill level. Since the early days, parents and friends have volunteered to help organize and sponsor the races. Now the love for BMX riding has gone beyond racing motos. Dirt riders have taken their jumps, tricks, and styles to the street and onto vert ramps, mini courses, and flatland (see p. 25).

NOT YOUR AVERAGE BIKE

With all the pounding on dirt courses and vert ramps, BMX bikes need to be built tough enough to withstand serious abuse. BMX bikes are smaller than other kinds of bicycles, with wheels 20 inches in diameter. The smaller bikes became standard mostly because the craze started out as a sport geared toward young riders. Keeping the bikes small was a way to even the playing field for kids of different sizes. BMX bikes are also free from extras that can add unwanted weight or slow a rider down, such as mudguards, reflectors, chain guards, and kickstands. Because BMX riders don't need to climb hills or sprint for long distances, there's no need for multiple gears. A single gear keeps the bike lighter and helps the rider focus on handling instead of shifting.

NOT YOUR AVERAGE RIDER

One thing that goes hand in hand with BMX riding is falling. A good rider will learn how to tumble out of a fall with a shoulder roll or forward roll. That may help absorb some of the shock of falling, but it still doesn't take the place of good protective gear. Whatever your style of BMX riding, you'll minimize injuries if you have a helmet, gloves, eye protection, and wrist, knee, and elbow guards. If you're going to be on the race tracks, you might be required to add padding to the frame and to the crossbar and stem of the handlebars.

So What's It Gonna Be?

Ever since BMX exploded in the '70s, waves of new riders constantly challenge the old school. Inspired by their heroes, they ride harder, jump higher, and invent new tricks to blow their friends away. The result? There are now so many ways to ride BMX that it may be hard to focus on only one style. So don't. Experiment with different styles. Discover what works best for you.

A BMX rider balances on the front wheel of his bike as the rear tire lifts behind him in a perfect table top.

IN THE BEGINNING, THERE WAS DIRT

Dirt track races throw riders around high-packed berms, jumps, and whoop-de-dos in a sprint for the checkered flag. It's fun to catch major air, but the key is smoothness on courses that combine single jumps, sets of doubles, sharp turns, downhill runs, and step-downs thrown at you at white-knuckle pace.

FREESTYLE THRILLS

Freestyle is a dazzling display of acrobatics on a BMX bike, combining balance, agility, and a reckless disregard for gravity. Different styles have emerged, but they all challenge common expectations of what's possible on a bike:

FLATLAND: Flatland removes the bike from tracks, jumps, ramps, or other props to bust it out on streets and in parking lots. It builds on the basics of the wheelie and bunny hop to do the near impossible—like standing 360s, squeakers, and tailwhips (see p. 27).

VERT: Vert riders execute awe-inspiring aerial gymnastics by using both sides of a half-pipe ramp to launch themselves high into the air. The higher they go, the more time they have to pull off their stunts. So these riders push it.

STREET/MINI: Street riders use curbs, stairs, benches, and handrails as their personalized jungle gyms. Mini is what you get when you take the street rider off the street and onto small courses featuring half-pipes, funboxes, and rails. Very similar to skateboard parks, these daredevil arenas can be found both outdoors and in.

VERBAL SKILLS

BERM: Dirt ridge formed around a turn by kicked up dirt.

HOT SHOEING: Sliding your inside foot on the ground during a turn.

LINE: The path a rider determines is the best option through a turn or other obstacle.

MOTO: One lap of a BMX race. Best two out of three motos wins the race.

QUARTER-PIPE: A curved ramp that makes the transition from horizontal to vertical.

HALF-PIPE: A ramp made of two quarter-pipes.

TABLE TOP: A type of ramp that features a long, elevated section after the transition that the rider can either jump over or onto. Also a type of stunt (see p. 27).

TRANSITION: The curve of a jump or ramp between horizontal and vertical.

WHOOP-DE-DO: One of a series of small ruts or bumps designed to slow the race pace.

20-INCHER: A term used to describe a BMX bike that refers to the diameter of a BMX wheel.

A quarter-pipe ramp will help this rider catch some air at the X Games in San Francisco.

Tricks 'n' Kicks

A rider flips over a stunt park. His bike is outfitted with pegs on the front and rear wheels.

Whether it's freestyle tricks at the X Games, or a neighborhood mini, there's no limit to how many ways you can pull stunts, combine them, and perfect your style.

You've seen the pros make the impossible look as easy as smiling. But they'll be the first to tell you that even the simplest of tricks takes practice—and a lot of it. Put on your helmet and a can-do attitude. You may not get it right the first time, but try, try again, and soon enough you'll be doing back-to-back tricks with the best of 'em.

STUNT PILOT

360: As you fly off a jump, turn your handlebars and head in the direction you want to rotate. Use your hips to throw your body weight into the turn, and spin with all your might to come back around full circle. Twice in a row, and you've done a 720.

TABLE TOP: Either off the lip of a ramp or in midair, pull up on the handlebars, cross them, and push down. At the same time, kick the back wheel up with your leg to lay the bike flat—like a table—in the air.

SUPERMAN: Glide off a jump, and pull a no-footer by straightening your legs behind you. Stretch your arms out front (still gripping the bars) as you fly through the air, superhero style, with your bike under you.

CAN-CAN: Think Rockettes, BMX-style. Cross one leg over the top tube of your bike frame and stretch it out. Be sure to bring it back before you come down for a landing!

CROSS-UP (X-UP): Whip out some fancy handlebar action when you jump by spinning your bars 180 degrees in one direction, then 180 degrees in the other, just in time to straighten out your front wheel for a touchdown.

NOSE PICK: A cool thing to do in front of your friends. Bunny hop into a controlled endo by hitting the front brake. With the rear wheel in the air, balance on the locked front wheel for a second. Then come back down onto both wheels.

TAILWHIP: Cross your right foot over the top tube and rest it on the front tire. Kick the pedal with your left leg to whip the frame of the bike around the front fork so that the frame travels 360 degrees while the front wheel stays stationary. Catch the bike with your left foot as it comes around, plant your right foot back on the right pedal, balance with your left, and you're good to ride.

SQUEAKER: With one foot on your front peg, hit the brakes and lean forward into a controlled endo. Position the other foot on your front tire, release the brakes, and scratch the tire backwards with your foot. Brake, release, scratch . . . brake, release, scratch. Keep on squeakin' as long as you can.

FUNKY CHICKEN: You've gotta see this one to believe it: Plant your right foot on the rear left peg while placing your left foot on the front left peg. Spin around the front of the bike on your left leg and start scratching the front tire forward with your right foot. Then rest your right foot on the top tube and grab hold of the seat. Flip the rear wheel up and scratch the front tire backward as you go around in a circle.

FAKIE: Do any stunt backward!

If You Build It...They Will Come

CLASS IS NOW IN SESSION

Unless you're only interested in flatland riding, you need the right tools to sharpen your skills. What if there aren't any tracks near you? Some stunt riders get around this problem by setting up their own courses, perhaps at school supervised by the athletic department, or at home in the driveway or backyard. Even areas of solid pavement can be made into fun courses by adding a few basic ramps.

TRAILBLAZING

If it's a dirt racing course you're after, start with an area that can hold at least a 1/8-mile loop. Create a starting area on an incline for quick starts off the line. Mix up your track with left and right turns. Build small berms around the turns to increase speed and cornering options. Frequent use will build them up. Break up the straight sections with jumps and whoop-de-dos. Raise the bar by adding sand or mud sections. Too many jumps can make the course unmanageable for racing. Instead, vary their height and style, and space them out so you have time to land before hitting a turn or another hazard. Build a jump by using a wooden base, such as logs, and covering it with at least four to six inches of dirt.

GO THE MAX WITH MINI

Mini courses can be set up on any paved surface. The basic building blocks of the mini section are the quarter-pipe, funbox, and rails. You can set them up in a variety of heart-pumping combinations and store them away when you're through. Quarter-pipes give you vertical height on a jump and are particularly good for stunts like 360s where you land back on the ramp. They're most often built with plywood and strongly braced to withstand a beating. Like the dirt course, more variety in shape and size means more fun for everyone. The funbox is a must-have for your mini. This incredibly versatile stunt platform has a square or rectangle top of varying height with curving ramps that spread out on all four sides.

FUNBOX

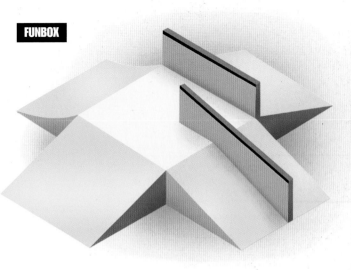

THE BACKYARD THRILL MACHINE

The granddaddy of all ramps—the half-pipe—is what you need for any serious vert session. Nothing beats it for huge air, and it can be built in small areas. The half-pipe looks like two quarter-pipes stuck together end to end to form a half circle, or oval. You should have a platform on the top at each side for riders to stand on with their bikes and a safety fence to prevent anyone from going over the edge. It's also good to have a flat section on the bottom before the transition to vert.

START SIMPLE

Can't build a ramp? No worries. Mark out a course with buckets or old tires. Try building small ramps out of plywood laid over cinder blocks. Create obstacles with metal or plastic pipes or logs spaced out on the straight sections.

Road Racing

- The Obsession
- The Racing Scene
- The Tour
- Need for Speed

The rush of the pack. The thrill of pursuit. The drama of reeling in the breakaway. Get it in gear because the road is calling you.

The Obsession

As the pack—known to racers as the peloton—carves the last turn of a switchback descent, the lead rider breaks away in an all-out sprint. What had been a single pulsating mass of cyclists splits in two as other riders break away from the pack to give chase, each hoping the others will blow out first and drop their pace. Welcome to the world of road racing.

Can a sport be an addiction? For many road racers, riding is an all-consuming experience. Depending on their competition schedule, racers can log hundreds of miles a week while training. Although elite professionals actually get paid to train, most riders have to juggle school or work with their cycling. That may not leave much time for other pursuits, but racers are rewarded by every second whittled off their best time.

BUILT FOR SPEED

If there's one thing all racers have wanted from their bicycles since the dawn of competitive cycling, it's speed. To make bikes faster, engineers have always explored ways to make them lighter. Today, a top-end racing bike can weigh as little as 18 pounds. These bikes are made of light frame materials such as steel alloys, titanium, and carbon fiber. Each of these materials has its own "feel" while riding, and most cyclists develop a preference over time. The shape of the tubes has also improved, with some frame designs using aerodynamic, wedge-shaped tubes to cut through the wind.

THE HUMAN ENGINE

The most important component on the bike is the rider. A racing position has the rider bent low over the handlebars with elbows and knees tucked in to reduce wind resistance while pedaling. No matter how light the bike is, it will only go as fast as its rider is able to push it. That means pushing yourself for extended periods of time to build endurance. You must constantly marshal your strength for the most efficient use of energy. Many racers describe a feeling of "becoming one with the bike" when they find the perfect combination of pace, effort, and speed.

TRAIN LIKE A PRO

EAT WELL: All that riding burns fuel. Eat complex carbohydrates, such as fruits and vegetables, for energy and lean protein, such as chicken or tofu, to build muscle.

CHART YOUR PROGRESS: Record the distance and time of all your training rides. Tracking your improvement helps keep you motivated.

FIND A GROUP: Riding regularly with a group of peers has many benefits. Camaraderie is half the fun! You'll want to ride more frequently, and you'll learn from exchanging tips and observing other riders.

RIDE HARD, REST HARD: In order to improve performance, you need to push yourself, but your muscles need time to rebuild as well. Try alternating hard rides with "recovery" rides at a more mellow pace, and occasionally take a day off.

DRINK UP: As you sweat, your blood becomes thicker due to water loss, and your heart works harder. This results in increased fatigue as well as the possiblility of sunstroke. Make sure you drink plenty of water before you ride and drink at least 1 pint (.5 liters) of water every hour during your ride.

The Racing Scene

Although there are many different styles of road racing, they all share one common factor: From team races to individual time trials, competitors pour every scrap of strength and determination into the quest to ride faster, ride smarter, and, they hope, to bring home the gold.

Cyclist Lance Armstrong, pictured at right, overcame cancer to win not just one but three consecutive Tours De France (1999, 2000, 2001). But every cyclist who makes the decision to race enters a brave new world of competition and camaraderie. No matter what place you finish, you'll probably never have ridden so fast in all your life. And chances are, you'll want to do it again.

Lance Armstrong competes in an individual time trial.

THE RACE OF TRUTH

Individual time trials pit racers against their most serious adversary: the clock. Instead of mass starts like other forms of racing, time-trial riders start alone in one-minute increments with the fastest riders last. Unable to pace themselves against other riders, the racers must rely solely on their mental and physical strength to be able to ride with speed and consistency. The rider who finishes with the fastest time wins. In the United States, the courses tend to be 25 miles (40 km) while European time-trials are longer, with 45-mile (72.5-km) courses. Because every second counts, time trial riders go to great lengths, such as wearing skintight body suits and tapered helmets, to reduce wind resistance. To further reduce drag, the bikes tend to have rear disk wheels, small front wheels, aero handlebars (see photo, above), and wedge-shaped frame tubes.

THE MAD DASH

Some of the most exciting races for spectators are the criterium races. These races have very short courses varying from .5-mile (.8-km) to 1.5-mile (2.4-km) loops. Racers may pass a spectator more than a hundred times during the course of a race, which can be from 25 miles (40 km) to 62 miles (100 km). These races are usually held in cities or parks to add to the excitement. Criterium races demand excellent bike handling skills as riders jostle for position during constant cornering and rapid bursts of acceleration. Crashes are common, and one rider can bring down a whole pack with a split-second error. Like time-trial bikes, criterium bikes have more aerodynamic designs than the classic road bike. Criterium races can be won several ways. Some races award victory to the first rider across the finish line, while others award points for each lap won.

TAKING IT TO THE LIMIT

Not content with regular stage, or point-to-point, races (see p. 36), some competitors feel the need to compete in ultramarathons featuring multi-day continuous racing over great distances. Perhaps the most famous is the Race Across America (RAAM), a 3,100-mile (4,989-km) race that tests the limits of human endurance. Racers must simply finish the course in the fastest time possible. Unlike stage races, this event is continuous, with no guidelines for sleep or rest. Most racers average about three hours of sleep a night and start each day from wherever they left off the night before. Roughly half the riders drop out, and those who remain generally finish the event in nine or ten days.

The Tour

Every June, an elite group of cyclists gears up for the most grueling event of the year and arguably the most challenging sporting event in the world: 21 days of the Tour de France.

At the turn of the 20th century, bicycle fever hit France. Track racing had been an established sport, but the new concept of road racing was only starting to become popular. Initially, road races were organized by newspaper journalists as a way to sell papers. In a flurry of competition between two French newspapers, journalists Géo Lefèvre and Henri Desgrange of the sports daily *L'Auto* dreamed up the race to end all races—an event that would be broken up into stages along the roads of France. Each day would comprise a single stage, ranging from a few dozen to more than 100 miles (160 km). In 1903, the first Tour attracted 60 riders; today, as many as 200 compete for the yellow jersey.

THE ROUTE

Every year, town councils and businesses vie for the chance to be included along the route of the world-famous race. The distance has varied from as few as 1,507 miles (2,425 km) to as many as 3,568 miles (5,742 km). Daily stages often cover more than 100 miles (160 km) and are seldom continuous. It's common for riders to transfer by train or airplane between stages. What stays the same? Killer climbs, screaming descents, critical time trials, and a test of endurance that lasts three weeks along roads lined with millions of cheering spectators.

THE RIDE

Top riders spend half a year or more preparing themselves physically and mentally for the Tour. No amount of solo training can prepare you for the psychology of riding in the peloton, or the pack. An animal unto itself, the peloton moves like a singular force. Riders line up in single file, or draft each other, mere inches apart. They pace each other and support each other. Team riders, known as domestiques, ride for the sole purpose of supporting their leader. They strategize to create key positions to maintain the lead, cut down on wind resistance, and avoid crashes. Every rider brings unique skills to the race—some excel in sprints, others in climbs, others in strategy. Knowing when to hold back and when to pounce can make the difference, edging a rider into the lead by a single, yet crucial, second. And even the best riders can be reduced to mush when beaten down by dehydration, fatigue, or the slightest miscalculation in shifting gears.

THE JERSEYS

YELLOW: This coveted jersey, seen below on Lance Armstrong, is worn by the rider with the best time after each stage. Ultimately, the Tour winner earns the privilege of parading the yellow jersey along the Champs Elysées, one of the grandest boulevards in Paris.

POLKA DOT: The challenge of charging up the Alps and the Pyrenees during the Tour's mountain stages can make or break the best riders. Faced with as much as 10,000 feet (3,000 meters) of pure uphill in one day, the pros can do it at average speeds of more than 20 miles per hour (32 kmph). If you see spots, you're looking at the best climber of the pack.

GREEN: Each stage includes an individual and team time trial, during which the riders give it all they've got in an all-out sprint. The rider who earns the most points per stage in sprints sports the green jersey.

Need for Speed

You never really know how fast you can go until you race. Even then, you'll go faster than you ever thought you could.

Nothing can top the rush of riding with the pack that's making a break for the lead. One taste of speed, and you may never ride your bike the same way again.

Road racing is more than simply riding fast. It's a blend of physical conditioning, skills, and frame of mind. As a racer, you need to remember that you're unique. You might be a speed-demon sprinter but need to work on making that energy endure in long-distance hauls. With differences in ability come differences in training and style. There's always more than one way to get up that hill, keep the pace, and finish strong. What works for you? There are some tried and true strategies.

SPRINTING

1. Blow off that steam by starting out in a slightly harder gear than necessary for the grade.

2. For an additional burst of speed, get out of the saddle, pull with your arms, and pump hard with your legs. Timing is key: As you push down with your right leg, pull on the handlebar with your right arm. Relax your right arm as you push down with your left leg and pull with your left arm. Alternate pulling and relaxing with each stroke.

3. Minimize wind resistance. Keep your elbows in, head down, and body square to the bike.

4. Avoid extending your legs all the way with each stroke. Pull up on the pedal with one leg as you push down with the other. Keep the strokes fluid and constant—jerky strokes result in too much energy loss.

GOING THE DISTANCE

1. Vary your speed. Break up long rides with sudden bursts of speed. Sustain the sprint for as long or as short as you like—just be sure to give it all you've got.

2. Add one long ride to your training schedule each week. The extra miles will help you increase and maintain your endurance.

HONKING IT UP THAT HILL

1. Take a stand. Get up out of the saddle and pull lightly on the handlebars. Upper body strength can help you make the grade.

2. Maximize your spin. Whenever possible, prepare for a hill by shifting to a higher gear and increasing your revolutions per minute (rpm). Higher (or harder) gears will allow you to grab more road per pedal stroke. Lower gears might seem easier, but ultimately they'll slow you down.

3. Repeat, repeat, repeat! To climb like the pros, practice. Find a hill and ride hard to the top. Coast down to recover, then do it again. And again.

TOWING THE LINE

Paceline riding is a surefire way to increase your speed, endurance, and climbing ability. A team of riders form a paceline, or echelon, by lining up behind the lead rider. The pros ride tight—no more than a few inches between each rider. The lead cuts the wind resistance for all the other riders, thus cutting down on their effort. After a while, the front rider switches to the end of the paceline and drafts off the last rider, while the second cyclist takes a turn at the lead. Paceline riders need to maintain consistent speeds. If gaps open up between riders, it will break the flow and cause riders to lose the benefits of drafting.

Extreme
Sports

Part 4

Fast-Track Racing

- Spin Cycle
- The Race Is On
- Hall of Fame

So you like to go fast? How about carving the banks of the velodrome at highway speed? Fast-track racers are the rockets of the bicycle world.

Spin Cycle

Some of the first American sports heroes were speed demons blazing around hand-built tracks in pursuit of glory. As in the days of ancient Rome, thrill seekers in the late 19th century flocked to public arenas to see their favorite athletes duke it out on the field. Instead of the gladiators' swords and shields, the weapons of choice were the first generation of track bikes. That great tradition continues today as racers use modern technology to constantly push the envelope of human propulsion.

Current track bikes resemble road bikes, but with several major differences.

These thoroughbred race machines have a fixed rear wheel instead of a freewheel. This means that whenever the rear wheel is spinning, so are the pedals, so forget about coasting.

Track bikes have no brakes and a fixed gear. The only way to slow the bike is by resisting the forward spin of the pedals with reverse pressure.

The shorter wheelbase—the distance between the two wheels—is for quicker handling, and the pedals are mounted higher for better clearance on the banked tracks.

VELO-DRAMA

It may seem surprising now, but at the turn of the century track racing was the most popular sport in the United States. Hundreds of thousands of Americans joined cycling clubs and organizations and attended races. The pure speed of the bicycle fueled the public's fascination with the sport. Charles M. Murphy became a national hero on June 30, 1899, when he sprinted for a mile behind a locomotive on a specially built wooden platform in 57.8 seconds. At slightly more than 60 miles per hour (97 kmph), this was faster than any automobile at the time!

LOOK MA, NO BRAKES

The track bike of today has evolved quite a bit from the "ordinary," the heavy, hard-to-handle machine first ridden in the 1870s. The ordinary's front wheel was huge and had the pedals directly attached to it. The much smaller rear wheel was about the size of a Frisbee. The ordinary was followed by the "safety" bicycle, which more closely resembles the bikes we ride today. Both wheels were the same size, and the pedals drove a chain connected to the rear wheel. Although a coaster brake was developed for recreational riders, racers developed a fixed gear with no brake.

BICYCLE BATTLEFIELDS

The first track racers rode on a wide variety of courses, but as the sport evolved, so did the track. Wooden tracks became more common, with fast straightaways and banked turns. Bicycle stadiums, known as velodromes, sprang up across the country, replacing the dirt tracks at fairgrounds. Some indoor tracks were constructed so events could be held without interference from the weather. Wooden tracks were designed to be taken apart and reassembled for specific events at indoor locations, such as Madison Square Garden in New York City. The standard outdoor track today is 1,092 feet (333 meters) around and is made from concrete with a smooth surface. The shorter the track, the higher the banks on the turns, with some as steep as 50 degrees to the horizontal. A racer has to maintain a certain speed on those banks simply to avoid slipping and falling down.

The Race Is On

For pure drama, white-knuckle suspense, and the sheer thrill of victory, track events are by far the fastest and most exciting forms of racing the world of cycling has to offer.

For purists, track bikes are the greyhounds of the racing world. A day at the races is an event unto itself. Spectators willingly pay high ticket prices to watch cyclists top speeds of 50 miles per hour (80 kmph). Massive crowds will pack the velodrome stadium to watch a variety of races—individual, team, points, sprints, time trials—that provide the ultimate challenge of physical and mental grit.

THE PURSUIT

Two riders start at opposite ends of the track and chase each other for distances between 2 and 3 miles (3,000 and 5,000 meters). The first rider to catch the other or finish the race wins the event.

THE MATCH SPRINT

This fiercely competitive 1,000-meter race (.62 miles) pits two to four riders against each other. Only the last 200 meters (.12 miles) are timed, which means for the first four-fifths of the race, the riders are jockeying for position. The lead cyclist during a sprint is at a disadvantage because of wind resistance. Sprint racers constantly try to force their opponents ahead of them simply to tire them out. Often, the riders will force their bicycles to a standstill, called a "trackstand," as a way to slip in behind their opponents. If a racer can draft off his opponent, he'll have much more energy toward the end of the race to break away and charge for the finish line.

THE KILO

One of the most popular time-trial events, the Kilo is an individual 1,000-meter race (.62 miles) against the clock. Racers don't compete with each other, so they don't need to employ competitive tactics or strategies.

It's a test of pure strength and brute force. World record times for the Kilo average more than 30 miles per hour (48 kmph).

KEIRIN RACING

Made popular in Japan, Keirin racing is a competitive, and grueling, international bicycle event. Riders follow a single motorcycle around the track in a vicious 1.2-mile (2,000-meter) sprint. Jockeying for position is critical, and riders are ruthless in their attempts to elbow out their opponents for the sweet spot behind the motorcycle. In the last lap, the motorcycle pulls off the track, leaving the riders to face the headwinds alone and peel out for the finish.

POINTS RACE

Thirty or more racers compete against each other in this high-paced action race. Often about an hour long, the points race isn't about the best time but the most accumulated points during the race. Riders accumulate points during several speed intervals and pack sprints. That many racers zooming around the track at speeds of more than 45 miles per hour (70 kmph) can be wildly exciting . . . and mind-blowingly dangerous.

Hall of Fame

Marty Nothstein

What does it take to be a champion? More than just great legs and hard training, winning consistently demands an unshakable desire to be the best. These cyclists may hail from around the globe and across time, but they all share a passion for the track that's made them heroes. Meet some of bicycling's track stars from yesterday and today.

Marshall W. Taylor

BRINGING HOME THE GOLD

A Pennsylvania native, Marty Nothstein thrilled the American cycling community when he became the first American to win Olympic gold in 16 years. His first-place showing in the match sprint at the 2000 games in Sydney, Australia, was no fluke, however. His record already included a number of national and international wins. He took the silver in the match sprint in the 1996 Olympic games and was the top-ranked male sprinter that year. His other wins have included World Track cup events, American Velodrome Classics, and the Junior National Track Cycling Championship. Nothstein was a member of the U.S. National Team in 1990 and from 1993 to 1999. He continues to compete in the United States and abroad.

THE FASTEST BICYCLE RACER IN THE WORLD

Bicycle racing hero Marshall W. "Major" Taylor was the second African-American world champion athlete after the boxer George Dixon. Taylor's sprints left the finest racers in the dust—no small feat at a time when racism threatened his opportunities even to participate in world-class events.

In 1892, 13-year-old Marshall Taylor got a job in an Indianapolis bike shop sweeping floors. To lure customers, he donned a military uniform with brass buttons and performed fancy bicycle stunts in front of the shop. People started calling him "Major." Before the year was over, the shop owner entered Taylor into his first bicycle race as a joke. To everyone's surprise—including Taylor's—he won. He turned professional in 1896 and went on to hold seven world speed records as well as world and American titles.

THE DIXIE FLYER

You'll find him on the walls of the New York Sports Hall of Fame and the U.S. Bicycling Hall of Fame. Bobby Walthour, Sr., was one of the world's fastest cyclists in 1927, when the sport attracted as much national attention as baseball. Called the Babe Ruth of cycling, Walthour was a monster on the velodrome. In the early days of six-day races at Madison Square Garden, Walthour rode 142 hours and covered 2,555 miles (4112 km). That was one of 14 six-day race titles he snagged. When motor-paced races—races in which a motorbike acts as a pace vehicle for riders behind it—became popular, Walthour destroyed his opposition, claiming every motor-paced title win in Europe. Walthour became almost as famous for his injuries as for his world championships. He earned an entry in *Ripley's Believe It or Not* for being pronounced dead six times during his racing career.

DOES ALL THAT WINNING EVER GET BORING?

With 24 German national championships under her belt, Petra Rossner is a force to be reckoned with in her native Germany and the world. Possessing a deadly combination of both road and track skills, she was the 2001 National Road Champion and took the gold medal in both the National Pursuit and Points races in Germany. She achieved Olympic glory in 1992 with her gold medal in the individual pursuit. She also took top honors in that event the previous year when she won the 1991 world championship. She continues to pursue track and road gold and competes on the Saturn racing team.

Petra Rossner

Extreme Sports

Part 5

C-X Biking

- Winter Warriors
- Down 'n' Dirty in the Mud
- Cyclo-Skill
- Putting It on the Line

Never taking no for an answer, cyclo-crossers defy the mud, streams, and hills of ultimate cross-country racing. If you're a 'crosser, you live by this credo: Everything's accessible.

Winter Warriors

In 1903, the French journalist Géo Lefèvre organized the world's first "cyclo-pedestrian cross country race." The event had more in common with cross-country running than cycling, but the idea caught on. Soon, hard-core Belgian and French cyclists took to the woods during the cold, wet, and muddy winter months. They'd ride alongside horses through muddy trails, across streams, and over fallen trees. When the trail became impassable, they'd carry their bikes and keep on going.

What got started as an extreme winter mud fest through the woods quickly became a great way for bicycle racers to stay in shape during the off season. By the 1940s, enthusiasts regularly devised obstacle-filled courses for impromptu races. In 1950, the sport finally came into its own. Paris held the first international cyclo-cross event. Jean Robic, winner of the 1947 Tour de France, became the cyclo-cross's first world champion.

CYCLO-MADNESS

For serious cyclists, cyclo-cross is the ultimate extreme biking experience. A typical course challenges racers to a grueling test of rough terrain, artificial barriers, mud pits, grasslands, near-vertical climbs and descents, thick woods, streams, and hurdles. Racers need to have more than technical skills; they need razor-sharp reflexes and the ability to make split-second decisions. 'Crossers need to know when to ride, when to run, when to shift, and which choice will be the fastest. More than any other bicyclers, cyclo-crossers need to be masters of bike-handling skills. In the course of a single race, 'crossers pedal at top speed, run up hills, jump over obstacles, carry their bikes, and leap on and off their bikes without pause.

EXTREME FITNESS

Cyclo-cross courses are typically one to two miles (1.6 to 3.2 km) in length and last about an hour. But don't be fooled: This sport isn't for the weak at heart. Cyclo-cross is one of the most intensely difficult forms of bicycle racing. 'Cross riding builds incredible cardiovascular strength in addition to physical strength. Everything you can do on a road bike or mountain bike becomes harder on a cyclo-cross course. Ultimately, 'crossers are master cyclists. If you do 'cross, you'll become faster, learn how to use your energy more efficiently, develop incredible handling skills, and get in the best possible shape for every kind of bicycling.

THE PITS

One of the main advantages for cyclo-cross racers is that they are able to change bicycles several times during the course of a race. Pit crews stand by, ready to swap a mud-encrusted bike with a clean one after each lap. These high-speed mechanics will change tires, fix brakes, replace chains, and take care of just about any bicycle breakdown that can happen on the treacherous course. Why would a 'crosser swap a muddy bike if it's still working? Because a super mud-gunked bike can weigh as much as 22 pounds more than it does clean! That's a lot of extra load to lift during an uphill sprint.

Down 'n' Dirty in the Mud

What happened when the first road racers took their bikes across the fields of France? Sliding down wet grassy hillsides and confronted by fallen logs, they became aware of the limitations of their road-specific bikes. Inspired by the thrill of cross-country freedom, riders began to experiment, hoping to get an edge over the difficult terrain. Tested by time and heavy abuse, a number of these modifications became standard in today's cyclo-cross bike.

WHEN THE GOING GETS TOUGH...

As you blast down the treacherous and boggy hill, mud spins off your front tire and splatters your face and torso. Your legs have been caked since the first straightaway. The scary thing is that the mud is building up on your wheel rims. If your brakes get jammed with mud, you're sunk. At the bottom of the hill, the track spills into a sudden left turn. You squeeze gently, and the brakes clamp down, scraping through the mud to bring some much-needed control to your ride. Because 'crossers remove their right hand first during a dismount, they often prefer to switch their brake levers so that the left lever controls the rear brake. Why use the rear brake instead of the front? It's easier to feather when your weight's forward.

TRICKS OF THE TRADE

Rounding the turn, your eyes focus on the hurdles stretched out ahead and then on the long climb that follows. You'll need to do a fast dismount for the hurdles and remount quickly for the climb. You shift to an easier gear, and at the last moment, your hand flies off the bar as you spring from the pedals and swing your bike up onto your shoulder.

Moments like these highlight the special nature of the 'cross bike. As the sport evolved, shifters moved from the frame to the handlebar ends so 'crossers could keep their hands on the bars at all times. Recently, 'crossers have begun using shifters integrated with the brake levers, but many veterans still prefer the older end-mounted variety for better crash survival.

TAMING THE RACE COURSE

Two obvious details separate a cyclo-cross race from a road event: the muddy course and the riders jumping on and off their bikes. Engineered to deal with the mud, cyclo-cross bikes use knobby tires. Unlike mountain bike tires, these knobbies are thin, mounted on 700 centimeter rims like those on a standard road bike. Many 'crossers also like to run fewer gears in the rear cassette (the combination of chain rings on the rear wheel). Fewer chain rings have more space between them, which allows greater mud clearance. 'Crossers can afford to lose a few climbing gears because they tend to run up the really steep stuff. Because of all the dismounting and carrying, 'cross bikes also need to be very light.

Bar End Shifters

Cantilever brakes

Thin, Knobby Tires

Cyclo-Skill

You're ripping down a hill at top speed. You round the curve at the bottom of the hill to find a humongous log blocking the trail. Problem? No way. You're a cyclo-crosser. You'll be off your bike, over the log, and pedaling away at top speed without missing a beat.

One of the single most essential skills of the cyclo-crosser is the high-speed dismount. When mountain bikers face obstacles too large to bunny hop or power over, they stop, dismount, carry the bike, remount, and continue pedaling. Cyclo-crossers can do the same thing twice as fast, without stopping, and with style. For a 'crosser, it's all about getting through the course in the best possible time. If running up that hill or over that barrier with bike slung over shoulder is faster than pedaling, then that's what they'll do.

1. DERRING-DO DISMOUNT

As you approach the barrier, slow down slightly by feathering the brakes. With your hands on the top part of the handlebar or the brake hoods (the top part of the brake levers), unclip your right foot and swing your right leg over the bike. Bring your right foot between your bike and left foot. At the same time, grab the top part of the bicycle frame, or the top tube, with your right hand. Make sure your left foot is detached from the pedal, lunge your right leg forward until it hits the ground, and start running as you simultaneously lift the bike.

Think ahead: What kind of grade are you facing on the other side of the barrier? Shift into the proper gear before you dismount.

2. SIZE MATTERS

Are you crossing a stream, a fallen tree, or a narrow gully? Simply lift the bike about waist high and leap over the obstacle in a step (or two) before remounting. What if you're facing a super-steep hill, an imposing artificial barricade, or knee-deep mud bogs? You'll need more clearance. Hook your right arm under the top tube and sling your bike over your right shoulder. Keep the front wheel straight by grabbing hold of the left brake hood with your right hand as you run.

3. REMOUNT & RIDE ON

Once you've cleared your hurdle, grab the brake hood with your left hand, and gently lower your bike back to the ground with your right hand while you're still running. Be careful not to bounce the bike! Timing is critical: As you leap off your left foot, swing your right leg back over the bike. Hop back into the saddle by landing on the inside of your thigh, then sliding onto the seat. Find your pedals, clip in, and charge.

Pedal position: Your pedals should be in the same position when you remount as you left them for your dismount. For optimum remount speed, make sure you unclip for the dismount with your right pedal at 12:00 and your left pedal at 6:00.

Putting It on the Line

Cyclo-cross races are heart-pounding, lung-bursting contests of skill and strength. They're held on short courses that are at least .6 miles (1 km), but are generally 2 to 3 miles (3.2 to 4.8 km) in length. Racers will complete a series of laps during the race. Some courses have paved sections, but courses are generally rough with a variety of surfaces and obstacles. About 75 percent of the course should be ridden, and the rest covered on foot. This sample course contains many of the elements a 'crosser must face during a typical race.

CRASH COURSE

1. The starting area is wide enough for a big group and long enough for the racers to string out before hitting the rest of the narrower course.

2. Arrows or rope keep riders on the correct path. After the beginning section, the trail narrows to no less than 7 feet (2 m) wide, so passing is always possible.

3. Obstacles aren't higher than 16 inches (40 cm) and are meant to make riders dismount.

4. Riders face natural hazards, such as mud or sand patches, as well as artificial ones, like stairs or wooden barriers.

5. Streams or dry gullies, popular obstacles, can't be wider than 1 yard (1 m) so racers can jump over them.

6. Depending on the event and weather conditions, pit crews may be allowed to assist the racers. Sometimes the course is so muddy that bikes need to be exchanged for clean ones after every lap.

7. Often racers confront steep hills that they'll charge up on foot. Even when it is possible to pedal up a hill, a 'crosser may decide it's faster to run.

START

PIT-AREA

STREAM

Bike Smarts

Riding well is about riding smart.
You have to know your limits if you want
to learn to exceed them. Respect
yourself, your bike, and your buddies.

Let the Good Times Roll

Sometimes we get so caught up in the thrill of riding that it's easy to forget there are others around us. Being aware of other riders is important, and remembering some basic "dos and don'ts" will enhance everyone's enjoyment of the sport.

ON SAFETY

1. Wear bright, reflective clothing if riding in bad weather or poor visibility.

2. Always tell someone where you're riding and for how long. Whenever possible, ride with a buddy.

3. Always wear a helmet. Make sure it's centered on your head and fits snugly for proper protection.

COURTESY COUNTS

Whether it is a road, trail, or track, blasting down your favorite course in record speed is an amazing thrill that can keep you smiling for days. Just remember that as rewarding as it is to push yourself to new levels of skill, there's also danger involved. Reckless riding can put both you and those around you at risk. A little bit of courtesy will minimize the hazards of riding and maximize respect for your fellow bicyclists.

- Ask first. During training rides on the road, don't draft a stranger without asking first.
- Inspire trust. Riding mere inches apart in a paceline is all about trust, so if you're pulling in the lead, call out hazards such as broken glass or potholes.
- Buddy, can you spare a tube? Offer

assistance to any rider who is hurt or has a mechanical problem. He or she will definitely appreciate it, and so will you when you get a flat miles from home.

- Keep it clear. If you must stop on a road or trail, move to the side to allow other riders room to pass through. Never stop just below a jump!
- Coming in for a landing! Call out jumps on crowded dirt jump trails to avoid crashing into others.
- Nice guys can finish first. Everyone wants to win the race, but avoid aggressive riding that can cause others to have accidents.
- Wait your turn. It can be dangerous and disruptive to enter a velodrome track when others are doing their laps, so wait until they've stopped.
- Space it out. If riding a trail with a group, keep at least two bike lengths between riders and more during downhill runs. It's bad to crash, but it's worse when your buddy runs over you and bites the dust, too.
- Share the trail. If riding a multi-use trail, respect the rights of pedestrians and equestrians. Slow down when you encounter them, and call out if you're coming up from behind.

Live to Ride

Every serious cyclist knows that no matter how keen the skills, no matter how trick the bike, no matter how slick the gear, a bike ride is only as good as the rider.

TRAIN, TRAIN, TRAIN

When Lance Armstrong isn't busy winning the Tour de France, he's on his bike training. Every single day. Even if you're a hard-core cyclo-crosser or BMXer and don't plan on riding the Tour any time soon, you'll be amazed at how much better you'll ride with a stronger, fitter body. Strength training can give your legs that extra oomph you need next time you're in for the long climb. Endurance training, like long-distance or cross-country running, will make the next long ride seem shorter. Speed training, such as high-intensity sprints, will help you shave crucial seconds off your best time. Here are some ways the pros stay in shape when they're not racing or at the X Games.

BEAT THE BONK

You know the drill: Eat a well-balanced diet, drink lots of water, get your z's. Whether you're dreaming of the mountain bike World Championships in Durango, Colorado, or the time trials at the next Olympic Games, it's never too soon to feed your body for the bike. A diet high in complex carbohydrates, such as fruits, grains, and vegetables, will give you more than just energy for your body. It also offers necessary vitamins and minerals to help your body make the most of that fuel. The best riders know that you should eat before you're hungry and drink before you're thirsty. But you can still hit the wall, even if you've eaten the right stuff and filled up with fluids before a ride. Carry water or sports drinks with you if you plan to be out for more than an hour. Ditto for food: An energy bar or a banana can keep you alert when your brain starts to fog.

CROSS-COUNTRY SKIING: An ideal winter alternative to bicycling that works many of the same upper-body muscles you use when on your bike. And there's inline skating—an excellent leg and cardio workout. Try it uphill!

RUNNING: One of the best calorie-burning cardiovascular exercises you can do. Break up your run with sprint intervals for added fitness benefits.

CALISTHENICS: Sit-ups, push-ups, and back exercises help strengthen the muscles that support your upper body while you're on your bike.

JUMPING ROPE: The faster you jump the better. A simple and quick way to put your motor skills to the test and bring out your inner speed demon.

The Saga Continues

Who to know, where to go, what to read, and how to get involved.

ORGANIZATIONS

American Bicycle Association (ABA)
P.O. Box 718, Chandler, AZ 85244
(480) 961-1903
www.ababmx.com

International Mountain Bicycling
Association (IMBA)
P.O. Box 412043, Los Angeles, CA 90041
(818) 792-8830

League of American Bicyclists
1612 K Street, NW Suite 401
Washington, DC 20006
(202) 822-1333
www.bikeleague.org

National Bicycle League (NBL)
3958 Brown Park Drive, Suite D
Hillard, OH 43026
(800) 886-BMX1
www.nbl.org

National Off-Road Bicycle Association
(NORBA)
One Olympic Plaza,
Colorado Springs, CO 80909
(719) 578-4596

United States Cycling Federation (USCF)
1750 East Boulder Street
Colorado Springs, CO 80909
(719) 578-4581

TRAIL INFORMATION

Bureau of Land Management (BLM)
U.S. Department of the Interior
18th and C Streets, NW, Room 1013
Washington, DC 20240

National Forests and Wilderness Areas
Forest Service
U.S. Department of Agriculture
12th and Independence Streets, SW
P.O. Box 2417, Washington, DC 20013

USGS Map Sales
Box 25286, Denver, CO 80225

NATIONAL REGISTRIES

American Center for Bicycle Registration
3030 N. 3rd Street, Suite 200
Phoenix, AZ 85012
(602) 241-8547

National Bike Registry
2100 Watt Avenue, Suite 110
Sacramento, CA 95825
(916) 972-1100

WEB SITES

Cyclo-cross.com
www.cyclo-cross.com

Geoff's BMX/Freestyle Land
www.bmxfreestyleland.com

USA Cycling Online
www.USACycling.org

Bicycling magazine
www.bicycling.com

Mountain Bike magazine
www.mountainbike.com

Transworld BMX magazine
www.bmxonline.com

ABOUT THE AUTHORS

Monique Peterson is the author of dozens of books and articles about art, animation, pop culture, science, history, health, sports, and technology. An avid mountain biker and roadie, she's had the pleasure of riding with world-renowned pros. She lives in Brooklyn.

Zachary Zimmerman has been a mountain biking advocate and gear junkie for more than a dozen years. He leads group rides in the northeast U.S. when he's not production managing music videos and commercials. Prior work also includes science and music writing as well as photography.

PHOTO CREDITS

PhotoDisc: Pages 2, 10, 12, 17, 38, 58, 61, 62, 63; Mike Powell/AllSport: Pages 4, 8, 19, 30, 40; Jed Jacobsohn/AllSport: Pages 6, 28; Anton Want/AllSport: Pages 7, 51; EyeWire: Page11; Photos courtesy of Cannondale: Pages 13, 53; Al Bello/AllSport: Page 14; AllSport: Page 15; Robert Laberge/AllSport: Pages 18, 19; Jamie Squire/AllSport: Pages 20, 47; Donald Miralle/AllSport: Page 22; Tom Hauck/AllSport: Page 23; David Leeds/AllSport: Pages 24, 25; Corbis Royalty Free: Pages 26, 27, 60; Matt Turner/AllSport: Page 32; Digital Stock: Page 33; Brian Bahr/AllSport: Page 34; Doug Pensinger/AllSport: Pages 35, 36, 37, 42, 45; Pascal Rondeau/AllSport: Pages 39, 54; Stephen Munday/AllSport: Page 43; Corel: Page 44; Mark Dadswell/AllSport: Page 46; Hulton Archive: Page 46; Vandystadt/AllSport: Pages 48, 50, 52 56

Copyright © 2002 National Geographic Society.
All rights reserved. Reproduction of the whole or any part of the contents without written permission from the publisher is strictly prohibited.

Library of Congress
Cataloging-in-Publication Data
Peterson, Monique.
Bike! / Monique Peterson, Zachary Zimmerman.
p. cm. — (Extreme Sports)
Summary: Explores various aspects of biking, including mountain biking, BMX biking, road racing, and fast-track racing.
ISBN 0-7922-6742-7 (pbk.)
1. Cycling—Juvenile literature. [1. Bicycles and bicycling.] I. Zimmerman, Zachary. II. Title. III. Extreme sports (Washington, D.C.)
GV1043.5 .P48 2002   796.6—dc21   2001052188

Series design: Jay Masoff
Design and Editorial: Jack&Bill/Bill SMITH STUDIO Inc.